The Magic of Who You Are

Sofia Eastmond

Illustrated by Elena Rae Pulido

Balboa Press books may be ordered through booksellers or by contacting:

Balboa Press
A Division of Hay House
1663 Liberty Drive
Bloomington, IN 47403
www.balboapress.com
1 (877) 407-4847

ISBN: 978-1-9822-2307-6 (sc)
ISBN: 978-1-9822-2306-9 (e)

Library of Congress Control Number: 2019902339

Print information available on the last page.

Balboa Press rev. date: 03/04/2019

BALBOA
PRESS
A DIVISION OF HAY HOUSE

In memory of Bethany Wildbore's free spirit.

May these words help create a world where we learn to honour our love over our fear every day. And may they remind every soul that reads them of who they truly are.

Above all, may they inspire us all to infuse our lives with kindness, passion and magic. Life's too short for anything else.

To my darlings Abi, Rosário and Isabella,
for inspiring me to be a better person every day.

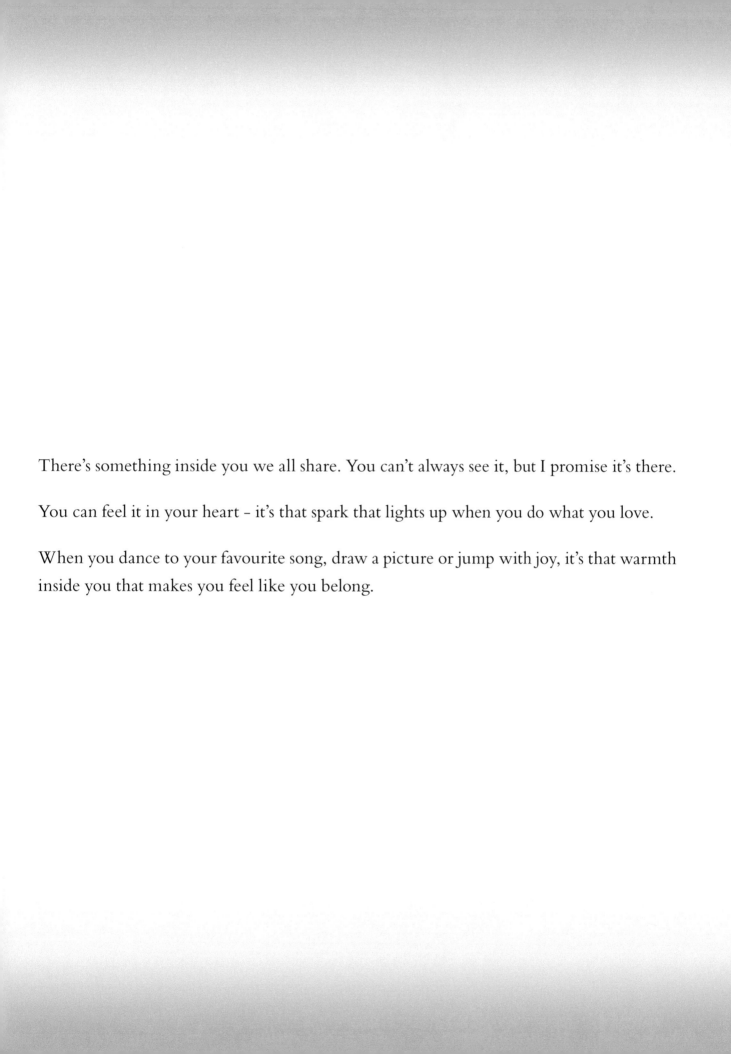

There's something inside you we all share. You can't always see it, but I promise it's there.

You can feel it in your heart – it's that spark that lights up when you do what you love.

When you dance to your favourite song, draw a picture or jump with joy, it's that warmth inside you that makes you feel like you belong.

That feeling is energy and that energy is love. We're all connected by it. It's all around us, below and above.

Even the animals and plants, the oceans and mountains share this light that beams inside you.

It's this love that creates all things good, as only that mighty power would.

It's the part of you that knows you're never alone, that you're a piece of something much bigger - this world we call home.

It's a light so mighty, that shows up as kindness, creativity and excitement. If you listen to it closely, it will always give you guidance.

We're all part of a big umbrella of light, with rays weaving everything together. In beautiful universal order, my story and yours are connected forever.

You're all the goodness and all the gifts. You're made of stardust and wonderful bits.

Let me paint you a picture: you're light, you're love and spark. And your body is the beautiful wrapping for this mighty power of the heart.

And there's another precious side of you…

Filled with big feelings and confusing thoughts that make up your wavy, stormy part. You're the ordinary and the divine dancing together in a magnificent piece of art.

Here's something important I need you to know. Feeling good, feeling bad; it's all part of it. Making mistakes too. It's what makes us human and sits right inside the magic in you.

No matter how big your upset, don't worry, you're powerful and you can handle it.

When life gets tricky, your light will always be there to show you a better way, look after your heart and wipe your worries away.

Let me tell you a secret: this light you're made of gives you magic powers.

You don't believe me? Give this a go… Next time you feel worried or need inspiration, close your eyes, take a deep breath and use your imagination.

Make a wish, say thanks in your heart and the universe will help you make a start.

For the universe (you might call it another name) will conspire with you and give you signs, like clues, of what you need to do.

It will always show you the way of kindness towards yourself and all living beings. Because love is what will mend the planet and its magical rhythms.

My darling, one more thing before I go… We're not what we do, you know?

So when you say or do something you're not proud of, that's okay. It doesn't take your awesomeness away.

We're all here to learn to forgive, love ourselves and each other more. So next time you're down, look inside your heart and you'll know what to do for sure.

Keep your light shining bright and look for the magic in others too. We're all in this together, in more ways than I can show you.

It won't always be easy, but I promise there is ALWAYS a way out. You're not alone in your journey. Together, you, your people and the universe will figure it out.

For the world is a wonderful place, in all its glory and mess, but the ways of the heart will show you your happiness.

So be who you truly are (the good, the average, the magic). Focus on your light and create a life that's your own version of fantastic.

Dear grown-ups,

This book is for you and me, as much as it is for our children.

So many of us have forgotten who we truly are and the world urgently needs us to remember.

Somehow, in the messy process of growing up, we've lost sight of how powerful we are. And we've forgotten how love, connection and creativity really are our natural ways of expressing ourselves in the world.

What better evidence can we find of this, than in our beautiful children? Look how naturally they're drawn to each other and the world around them… It's a real miracle to witness.

My wish is that they never forget their inner spark, their connection to a bigger power and the impact they can make in the world. And that we, adults, rediscover this for ourselves too.

So often we allow our fears to speak higher than our love. We hold our words back, we take life for granted and fall into the trap of leaving what lights us up in the "one day, maybe" pile.

Only you know what lights you up, and it's often the small things. Today is the day to pick up the pen, or that guitar or use your voice. Whatever it is, what are you waiting for?

Sure, there's enough mess in the world, but only our light can show us our way out of it and bring joy and excitement back into our lives.

There was once a time when we believed anything was possible. Well, it still is. We just forgot how to breathe into our courage, lean into what matters to us and ask for the help we need to make it happen.

Equally, we've forgotten that life is supposed to be stormy and wavy and that we're born with an innate ability to navigate it. With our inner compass in hand, our conviction of our role as co-creators of our own lives and our communities, there's nothing we can't handle.

May we step into our power to face the shadowy part of life with courage and an open heart. May we feel what we need to feel fully and resist the temptation of numbing ourselves.

And may we do it together, without our masks on, so we can be the demonstration, especially to the young people around us, of this resilience and connection, so that they don't unlearn theirs.

Let's lose our fear for each other and recognise in each other our humanity and our divinity, with a deep understanding leading the way.

May our love serve our world. And may our gifts be expressed in it. Sometimes all it takes is a few small steps in the direction of the heart… Of surrendering our *shoulds* to our dreams, one action at a time.

With my love, gratitude and recognition,
Sofia Eastmond

Printed in the United States
By Bookmasters